ONE HUNDRED WAYS TO

Live with a
Dog Addict

◈

ONE HUNDRED WAYS TO

Live with a
Dog Addict

BY
Ronald Payne

ILLUSTRATIONS BY
Jilly Wilkinson

Hodder & Stoughton
LONDON SYDNEY AUCKLAND

Text copyright © 2005 by Ronald Payne
Illustrations copyright © 2005 by Jilly Wilkinson

First published in Great Britain in 2005

The right of Ronald Payne to be identified as the Author of
the Work has been asserted by him in accordance with the
Copyright, Designs and Patents Act 1988.

1

British Library Cataloguing in Publication Data
A record for this book is available from the British Library

ISBN 0 340 90854 8

Typeset in Baskerville by Avon DataSet Ltd,
Bidford-on-Avon, Warwickshire

Printed and bound in Great Britain by
Bookmarque Ltd, Croydon, Surrey

The paper and board used in this paperback are natural recyclable products
made from wood grown in sustainable forests. The manufacturing processes
conform to the environmental regulations of the country of origin.

Hodder & Stoughton
A Division of Hodder Headline Ltd
338 Euston Road
London NW1 3BH
www.madaboutbooks.com

Love and respect to my wife Celia Haddon for critical guidance; and to her sister, Jilly who knows everything about dogs, yet still loves them.

Contents

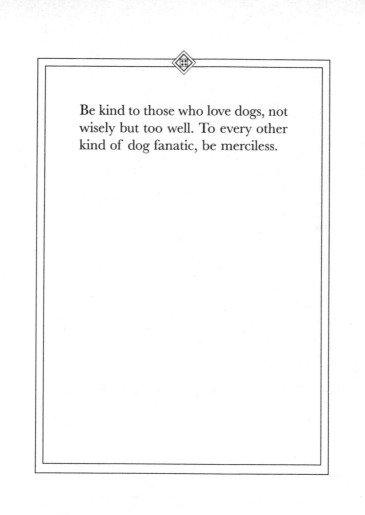

Be kind to those who love dogs, not wisely but too well. To every other kind of dog fanatic, be merciless.

Introduction

The ideal dog addict is warm-hearted and understanding, full of low cunning and has the addiction-fuelled ability to lie convincingly. Not all aspiring carers are so gifted . . .

This book suggests ways to keep canines and humans living together in reasonable contentment, and aims to bring comfort to those doomed to live with addicts. The addict carers' task is to help feckless individuals who slide over the ill-defined border between natural affection for dogs and fatal addiction to them. In the caring industry such unfortunates are known as *Doggios*.

Pre-emptive Techniques

Certain advanced techniques may be recommended to forestall the introduction of a canine into the household before any damage is done.

As soon as dog acquisition is first mooted, be ready to stress the complications of ownership.

Point out the awe-inspiring range of choice. There are as many breeds of dog as there are kinds of cheese in France.

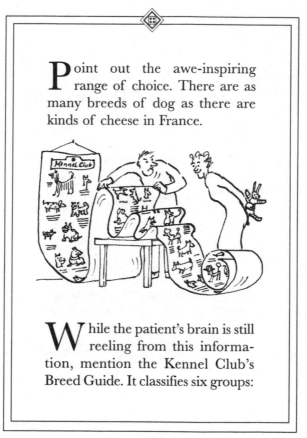

While the patient's brain is still reeling from this information, mention the Kennel Club's Breed Guide. It classifies six groups:

gundog, utility, terrier, working, hound and toy. Clouds of obfuscation may easily be created by using this official material in protective debate.

Your soft-hearted prospective addict is likely to be repelled by the mention of guns. A 'working' dog – a reminder of beer, tobacco and dodgy jokes – may seem socially unsuitable, 'utility' unexciting and 'toy' condescending in a trans-species context. There is plenty of scope for warding off trouble.

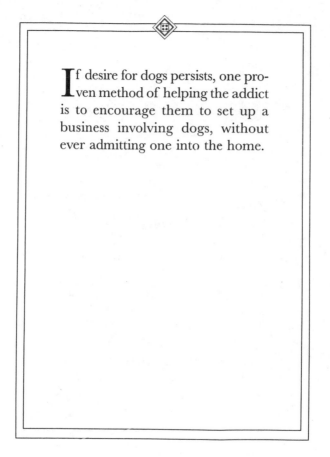

If desire for dogs persists, one proven method of helping the addict is to encourage them to set up a business involving dogs, without ever admitting one into the home.

A popular solution is to found a small company and name it Hire-a-Dog, 'provider of superior canines for all occasions, weddings a speciality'. This concentrates the mind on innocent money making. The animals responsible for the addiction come to seem far less important.

Becoming an Alpha Dog

All dogs are involved in a perpetual struggle to assert their own hierarchical power. Every dog must be either a pack leader alpha or an oppressed omega. If humans, through love, allow themselves to join the pack, they had better watch out.

If you don't look sharp, you'll end up an omega and a hairy German Shepherd will take your place on the double bed, leaving you cowering in the guest room.

Dog addicts come in two forms – alpha and omega. The alpha addict (of either sex) commands the pack with ceaseless vigilance, constant patrolling, and a stream of instructions in a dominant and manly voice.

If you live with an alpha addict, you will become part of the pack overnight. Do not answer back. It

will be to no avail. This will only be
tolerable if you have a high degree
of innate submission and enjoy
taking orders.

The omega addict is way down at the bottom of the pack hierarchy. A human omega feeds her dogs before she herself eats and races to gratify their every wish. The omega addict is usually badly dressed and unable to care for herself. Make yourself pack leader and start telling her and the other dogs what to do. This relationship role would suit a retired sergeant major or traffic warden.

Don't believe everything you read in old-fashioned dog training books. There is no need to cram yourself into dog baskets trying to prove you are *de facto* pack

leader, or to crouch over the dog's food bowl pretending to munch dog food, so as to control the pack's resources. Instead, ignore the dogs with lofty disdain, pushing them away as they fawn upon you. This method will probably work with the dog addict too – though it might result in punch-ups with the alpha type addict.

Dog-maddened people have infiltrated four-pawed agents in key positions. There are army dogs (Commandos and Paras, naturally), and police dogs; dogs serve in drug squads, emergency rescue and bomb-sniffing teams. We are all at risk! If you are challenged by a police dog, demand to see its badge and mention human rights.

Getting Down to Basics

Do not forget that behind every jolly, laughing Rover lurks the gloomy threat of big canines crunching bones. For people forced, through human relationship or marriage, to live cheek by jowl with canines, it is well to be aware of this fact, however painful it might be.

It may prevent suffering simply to avoid contact altogether with the following:

A Rottweiler with a spiked collar
A Scottie wearing a tartan jacket

A woman addict whose dog has just
   died

Car stickers provide a useful
early warning system of addiction:

My best friend has a wet nose
Dogs are not the whole of our life,
   but they make it worthwhile
Show Cavaliers in transit
Slow down for puppies

At the first sign of addiction in
the household, keep the sus-
pect under close observation. The
next   recommended   immediate

action is damage control, followed
by a crash programme to divert
attention away from dogs.

Do not use children as a diver-
sion. They are not good enough
substitutes for dogs.

Make sure that people who love dogs too much are kept well away from rescue centres where appealing animals are offered to 'good homes'. The overwhelming urge to rescue can prove too much for them.

Puppies, with their juvenile, extra-cuddly charms, represent a special danger. A litter of them in the rescue shelter may cause domestic disaster. Suggest that a mature dog has a far greater need for a home, while highlighting the probability of younger animals peeing on valuable carpets and treasured objects.

If an endearing puppy photograph captioned 'Who will save me?' or 'Rescue me' appears in a newspaper, burn the paper fast.

It is pointless to forbid the use of mind-numbing endearments like 'Who's my beautiful, good little doggie-woggie?' If anyone close to you starts talking to dogs, using phrases such as 'Who is mummy's good little boy?', remember they are sick people.

Master the art of appearing to listen without hearing or reacting. Dogs do this all the time. So can you.

Should your companion dog worshipper say, 'Let's not go to the party, Chump will be upset if we leave him behind,' it is time to consider starting to build a life of your own. Self-care is essential when living with an addict.

Addicts make excuses into an art form. 'He's only playing,' uttered as the great beast places paws on your shoulders or his muzzle in your crotch, is a sure indication of frantic dog commitment.

Smoking gun evidence of addiction: as the guests go in to dinner they notice a belching, snoring hound in a basket and a large salad where the meat should be. The host utters in tones of admiration, 'Who's a naughty doggy?', with no thought for the hungry.

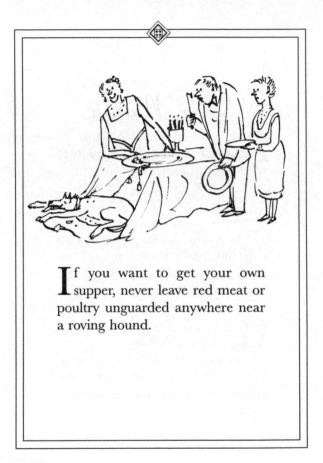

If you want to get your own supper, never leave red meat or poultry unguarded anywhere near a roving hound.

Dog Mania Can Damage Your Home Life

Always be on the alert for the first external signs of increasing dog dependency.

Watch out for any attempt to dress dogs in human clothes. Warm coats are permissible in extreme weather, though sledge-

pulling Husky dogs manage without. Pretend uniforms, Santa Claus
outfits, football strip, or naff baby
clothes are not.

Check your companion's will well in advance. It's only a question of time before your smart urbanite dog gets a serious paw on the property ladder. Max, Rover, Fifi and Miranda are waiting impatiently to get their sticky paws on family fortune and property. There are already plenty of old ladies who leave their houses and money to dogs, and even to cats!

Draw up a premarital agreement on dog ownership. Lawyers have started to regard companion animals as family members. Expensive alimony arrangements may loom. Worse still are divorce

settlements which leave you with custody of fourteen dogs.

Beware of people close to you who talk to dogs on the telephone. More to be feared are partners who leave messages for them on the answerphone. If your loved one starts texting the family dog, the end is nigh.

Be on the alert, both at home and in other people's territory, for telltale signs of dog infestation. You will immediately notice excessive supplies of dog leads, dog head collars, packs of treats, bottles of food supplements, winter clothing and enough bags of dried food to last through a siege. Be careful not to fall over special beds, heated rugs and canine toys.

In a typical dog-infested encampment, coffee tables will be littered with piles of books full of arty pictures of dogs. Technical works on the breeding of dogs and whelping manuals may jostle for space with award badges and trophy silverware. Every item should carry a warning – Here Be *Doggios*.

Give up all thoughts of a lawn with those enviable green stripes. Try to enjoy the interesting pattern of small brown holes left by your companion's favourite bitch.

Strategic placing of plastic bottles half-filled with water is the traditional way of keeping dogs from lifting their legs on rock garden conifers and other specimen garden plants. The bottles look worse than the dying plants.

Consider the possibilities of a Japanese sand and rock garden – no plants, just shifting patterns of sand. Paw marks could signify a Buddhist meaning and the turds are easy to pick up.

Dog hair on the carpet, the sofa, the sheets, and in the bath is inevitable. Stop fighting it. Make use of it. Spun with 50 per cent sheep's wool it turns into a yarn suitable for a wide variety of fashion garments.

Knit a golden retriever sweater, a dachshund woolly hat or a pair of Cavalier King Charles gloves. This will make a nice Christmas present for your dog addict. The owner can have a dog and wear it.

Defensive Actions

Consider lobbying for the Companion Dog Bill (Limitation of Numbers in Household) Programme. A return to dog licensing might go some way to producing the same result. Enjoy the irony that dog welfare organisations may appear as unlikely allies.

Castrate early and castrate often to foil any attempt by your addict to start dog breeding at home,

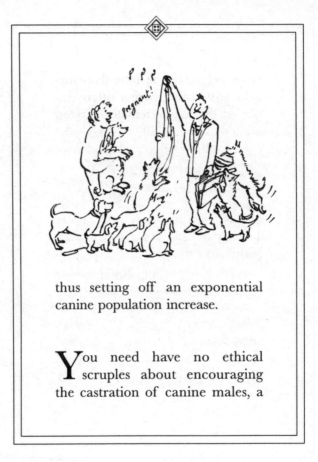

thus setting off an exponential canine population increase.

You need have no ethical scruples about encouraging the castration of canine males, a cause helped by the natural fascination with this process often displayed by human females. If your addict is a male, call in the vet, who is naturally keen on taking a fee for the snip.

Spay early and spay often. There may be opposition from women addicts keen on the biblical injunction to go forth and multiply, but any measure, however desperate, is acceptable to prevent living space being eaten up by litters of puppies. Bend feminist philosophy to insist, 'It is so unfair on canine mothers. She'll be worn out, poor bitch.'

Rare or new breeds of dogs are a temptation to dog dependants. The most alarming dog addicts by far are those whose life work is supervising stud farming of these creatures. The next step into deeper addiction is a pressing desire to display their creations at dog shows.

Dog shows are the equivalent of crack cocaine for dog dependants. Keep your addict well away from them. It's shocking the way dog show folk primp and preen their unhappy animals – even brushing the hairs on their little 'tassels'. They comb, shampoo, and perfume hairy dogs' bodies, turning them into something they were not meant to be.

If your addict sinks lower and starts hanging out with show people, there is not much scope for positive action. There's no people like show people, like no people I ever want to know people. At the merest mention of *Best in Show*, run for your life.

Choose the Brand, Choose the Name

You can't stop an incoming canine, but you can assert your right to influence the choice of breed. Try to make sure your addict's pet comes from designers you can trust:

Retired Greyhounds: worldly, tired of running
St Bernards: handy with brandy
Bloodhounds: sleep a lot
Sheepdogs: used to obeying orders

Never give a dog a bad name. To permit anyone to call what is meant to be a companion animal Terminator, Killer or Genghis Khan is to invite trouble. Either human minder or canine – sometimes both – will take on characteristics of the name. Other unsuitable stagey names, such as Juliet or Othello, usually lead to embarrassment. Keep names short and simple.

Any dog walker quickly discovers that the smaller the dog, the more exercise it takes and demands. Really big dogs tend to be lazier and therefore less demanding. Unless you enjoy a long hike, persuade your addict to get a big breed.

If children, wives, husbands and assorted partners must have a dog, suggest getting one from a dogs' home. It's cheaper, better for all

concerned, and a discouragement to the unpleasant backstreet trade of breeding for sale. The only drawback occurs if your addict develops rescue mania and abandons a well-paid job to become a kennel attendant.

H ard-pressed addict handlers will find it useful to remember that if the import proves unsuitable, dogs' homes will take it back (a useful loophole). Salve any pangs of conscience by making a generous donation to the organisation concerned.

A Firm Hand on the Leash

In the matter of training, addicts themselves are divided equally into the 'whack 'em's' and the 'train through rewards' pack. Some brandish sticks, others hold out proverbial carrots in the form of dried liver treats. Those involved in addict treatment do well to stay neutral on doctrine – not always an easy task. Those who train dogs tend to be fierce in their opinions, even when they are gentle with dogs.

Steal a trick or two from the more enlightened dog training manuals. For example, use kindly facial expressions and body posture, and be clear in your commands.

A dapt manual-speak whenever you address a dog addict, and be sure to reinforce each command with hand, arm or body signals.

K ind facial expressions and body language with clear commands are particularly important when shouting 'Get that bloody dog off the dining table!' An appropriate body signal is not a kicking motion of the leg (unkind body language) but a wide sweep of the arm as if clearing the table surface.

Dog trainers advise keeping sessions short – three 10-minute sessions are better than one 30-minute one. Always end on a good note: ask your addict to do something they are good at, like making the coffee or answering the telephone, and reward them well.

Stop addict training sessions when you feel yourself getting frustrated or angry, which is only too easy when you are trying to talk sense to such people. Otherwise you will pass these negative feelings on to the patient.

Praise and reward correct actions immediately. For turning down the offer of an 'adorable' puppy flowers, Belgian chocolates or an afternoon's shopping would all be suitable prizes.

'Make training sessions fun!' say the experts (they must be joking!). 'Like their pets, dog enthusiasts are born to play.' So if the session is fun, they will be more likely to learn and remember how to kick their addiction.

Play rewards could include a night at the opera, a country weekend, or drinks at a smart bar.

Continuing the play theme, try offering your partner's mobile phone to the dog, with encouragement to bite it like a bone. Don't forget to reward the dog for chewing up the item. Then praise your partner when she/he thoughtfully says: 'I've decided not to get a second dog until Bertie is behaving better.'

Beware the Winning Ways of Dogs

F ew people, least of all innocent children, are immune from the peril of being led into addiction by the winning ways of dogs.

Dogs possess legendary skills in making themselves loved – and obeyed. Stay clear of emotional manipulation.

Avoid unleashing a surfeit of truth by remarking, 'You care more about that dog than you do about me.' You may well hear things you do not want to. 'Bruno is a perfect friend – he never nags or answers back and I can tell him my worries. He is always sympathetic.' Unlike certain people!

When watching a person's helpless decline into dog dependency, remember the motto: 'There, but for the grace of dog go I.'

Alas, if your addict does hit rock bottom there is no DDA, or Dog Dependants Anonymous, with dog-free meetings and self-help style confessions. The only way you can help your addict is to keep this psychological illness at bay.

Never forget how easy it is to project thoughts and emotions that you feel it ought to have onto any adjacent canine.

All dogs display special skills in alleged understanding. Dogs listen as intently as a highly-paid therapist, offering unconditional support and unjudgemental attention, all for free. And they never talk back.

Alternative interests, such as:

a) girls
b) work
c) the pub and
d) real life

will help keep you, the addict's companion, relatively sane.

There's No Smell Like Dog Smell

Love may well be blind. Love of dogs demands an additional impediment that the companions of dog owners must be prepared to tolerate – a tragic inability to notice unpleasant odours connected with the animals.

It is an inescapable truth that most dogs emit evil smells all the time. Whether wet, dry, groomed, un-groomed, in sickness or in health, they smell strongly of dog. To everyone, that is, except dog-worshippers – they themselves are thankfully unaware that, through close association, they too smell strongly of dog.

For men and women with sen-sitive noses the best plan is to avoid partners or prospective soulmates already attached to, for instance Irish Water Spaniels. These otherwise splendid beasts, coated like shaggy hennaed sheep, are particularly fond of plunging into stinking pond water.

At all times keep your distance. For most dogs, their main enjoyment is to roll in excrement deposited by other animals.

A dditional excitement in the perfumery department can be achieved by rolling over in the smelly mortal remains of a dead sheep or rabbit. They even enjoy munching the stuff and then licking your face.

K eep at the ready a power hose, capable of producing a jet of cold water powerful enough to sluice off large chunks of evil-smelling debris from shaggy coats.

S trong coal tar disinfectant soap helps to ward off noxious smells.

Small dogs such as terriers may be easier to clean. That virtue is offset by the fact that they can be too quick to catch. They can also get dirty faster by other means, such as tunnelling.

A ccept the truth – most of the
time dog addicts smell like
dogs. Gifts of expensive perfume
can help a bit. Perfumery can trans-
form your addict and make her/
him smell of *eau de chien*, rather than
plain dog lavender water.

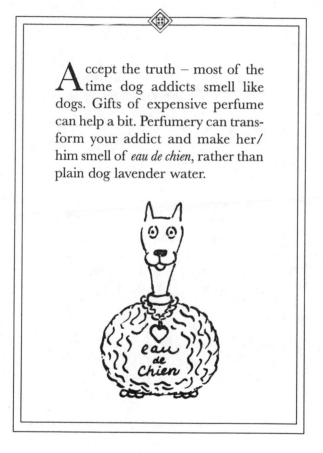

Recreational Dog Use

Though you live with a dog addict, you yourself can be classified, of course, as only an occasional, recreational dog user. Occasional dog use helps you to live happily with your addict.

Although in less politically-correct times the dog was known as man's best friend, women have a special bond with their pets.

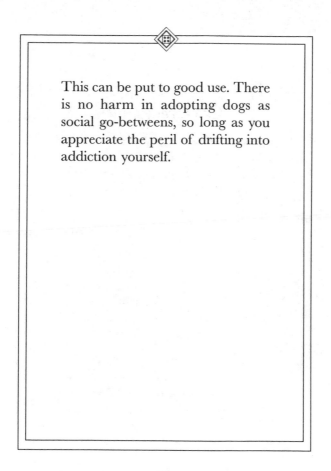

This can be put to good use. There is no harm in adopting dogs as social go-betweens, so long as you appreciate the peril of drifting into addiction yourself.

U se dogs as a password into the chat rooms of the kingdom of the addicts. It's a failsafe procedure for making social contact with addicts simply to say, 'What a lovely/obedient/well-trained/beautifully groomed/clever dog you have there!' Dogs may be used legitimately by both women and men for initial contact-making during skirmishes in the sex wars.

A word of caution about gender identification: a quick scan of the shaggy four-legged ones may not reveal for sure to the amateur dog spotter which dog is a Mr and which a Miss. When using dogs as conversation starters, avoid use of he or she until the owner has confirmed. Either can offend.

Show off your foreplay techniques. Gently fondle the ears
and head of an Afghan owned by
the most attractive woman in the
room. 'Look at the effect my loving,
sensual fingers are having on this
dog' is the message transmitted. The
signal may be reinforced by intense
eye contact across the room.

Doggy Paradox

Rule One of the living-with-an-addict warning code – never forget that you are dealing with a wolf in dog's clothing! That is the Doggy Paradox.

To watch a dog off the leash galloping across a riverside meadow chasing after a stick thrown by its owner is indeed a pleasing experience. What fun, you think, ready to join in the game. As he bounds towards you, it may be

too late already. 'He wants to be friends,' shouts the owner. In seconds paws are already punching at the most painful areas of your anatomy.

The correct defence against a jumping-up dog is to fold your arms, avert your gaze and turn your body quickly so that the paws land on your well-padded backside. Do not even look at the dog until its four paws are all firmly on the ground at the same time.

Take no notice when your addict says: 'Growling is his way of saying hello.' Do not put down your

hand for him to sniff unless you want to lose your fingers. Instead, find something very interesting at the far end of the room and slowly and carefully walk there to inspect it.

Casual feeding of somebody else's dog is a *faux pas*. Some addicts may solicit food for their dogs. If so, throw it to the ground – do not risk eager doggy jaws ripping it out of your grasp. Other addicts, if you are so unwise as to offer food, indignantly explain that their dog is on a carefully balanced diet.

Never try to separate fighting dog addicts. You are likely to become the target of transferred verbal aggression from both sides.

Never try to separate fighting dogs – unless you happen to be wielding a power hose or a Kalashnikov assault rifle.

Walking Your Addict (and Friend)

Classify as red-alert danger signals such seemingly innocent remarks as, 'I can't imagine anyone going for a walk without a dog.' This is a small step to 'I can't imagine anyone going on holiday without their dog', or even 'Imagine anyone going shopping without their dog.'

You will never be alone with your dog addict. Where they go, their dogs are sure to come along too.

B e aware that walking with a dog addict correctly inevitably involves the indignity of carrying small plastic scoops to gather up doggy excretions into little plastic bags. The bags then go into metal containers where they mature for months before collection.

W orse still, some dog addicts pick up the poo, put it in a bag and then tie the bag to a nearby tree like some primitive offering to the woodland spirit. Remarkable odours emanate from such places. Canines thus convert their humans into walk monitors and lavatory attendants. Human addicts rarely notice their new and diminished status.

Offering to take your addict's dog or dogs for a walk by yourself is also a mistake. The canines will either pull your arms out of their sockets, or race off into the far distance chasing rabbits.

Dog dependants are convinced, against all evidence to the contrary, that dogs are good for you.

Specially trained canines are taken to visit lonely old people. The effect is said to be therapeutic, though not all residents of care homes would relish being pawed and snapped at by a red-eyed Dalmatian with doubtful professional qualifications and dodgy teeth.

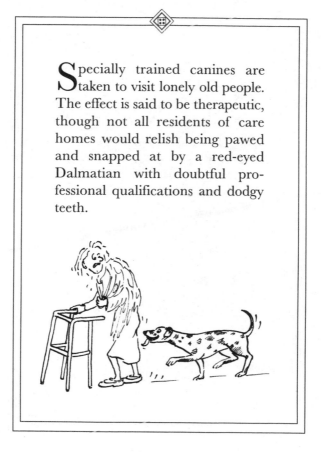

Do not let your addict anywhere near a pram. The final stages of dog addiction often result in the addict pushing a dog in a pram – hateful for the dog and hugely embarrassing for those seen with the addict.

Finally

When all else fails take advice from your dog. As Plato, the Greek thinker, wrote in *The Republic* – 'your dog is a true philosopher'.